SPIRITUALITY
A-Z

EXPLORING SPIRITUALITY WITH PRACTICAL
GUIDES FOR EVERYDAY

SPIRITUALITY
A-Z

Spiritual Awakening Guide for Healing
and Transformation

PATRICIA G. JOHNSON

ARPress
ILLUMINATING IDEAS
EMPOWERING VOICES

ARPress
45 Dan Road Suite 5
Canton MA 02021

Hotline: 1(800) 220-7660
Fax: 1(855) 752-6001

Ordering Information:
Quantity sales. Special discounts are available on quantity purchases by corporations, associations, and others. For details, contact the publisher at the address above.

Printed in the United States of America.

ISBN-13:   Paperback   979-8-89676-002-3
              eBook   979-8-89676-003-0

Library of Congress Control Number: 2021914440

Table of Contents

Dedicated to:

Al, Kristen, Richard, Chase & Francine;

My Inspirations.

Foreword

This book is written to honor all who are in various stages of recovery from life's events; including the International COVID Pandemic. These physical and/or emotional events have attempted to adversely halt our enjoyment of today and possibly prevent us from becoming the true self we are meant to be. Your resiliency and and commitment have taught me that spititual practices build a love and appreciation, compassion and kindness in ourselves for all living things; including ourselves. Spiritual practices give a tangible way to show appreciation for all that has been given to us by God.

I encourage you to approach this book with an open mind and willingness to try the various practices suggested. Consider its use as a beginning tool for your apiritual tool kit or arsenal of defense to assist on your own personal journey of healing and transformation. God bless you on your journey.

Patricia G. Johnson

WHY SPIRITUALITY?

A – Z Reasons with Guidance Practices

CKNOWLEDGE GOD"S PRESENCE in all to hold secure the connection to the invisible vertical AXIS which guides upward and reminds us to remain focused on higher values. Values that direct us to become the true person we are meant to be.

Practice: ASSESMENT of current spiritual direction: Ask what is my relationship with God and to myself? Write the answers. Give a brief history of your spiritual journey. You may be surprised at how many spiritual practices you currently use. Also, allow gaps in your spirituality to point the way to enriching your spiritual journey.

Practice: ACCOUNTABILITY PARTNER– working with someone to assist in honestly sharing struggles: to point out blind spots, choices or priorities that prevent us from moving forward towards our goals.

Practice: AMENDS – Promptly apologize and admit to mistakes and clear up misunderstandings even/especially if you didn't intend there to be a conflict or if the other misunderstood your words.

Practice: ACCEPTANCE – of persons, places and things – 'That's the way it is' – beginning with ourselves; as neither good, bad, nor ugly, but as perfectly made in the image of God. To postpone making judgements about others' motives, intentions or actions without the facts save us tremendously from harmful conjecture and speculation.

Practice: AUTHENTICITY – to seek honestly and courageously the source of conflicting emotions, such as anger, jealously, revenge, resentments and holding onto grudges. Recognize that these emotions may be masking sadness, hurt, or trauma: which can prevent us from being the true person we were meant to be.

Reflection

_____

_____

_____

_____

_____

_____

-**ELIEF** in something not seen, but deeply felt.

Practice: BIBLE STUDY – to determine how God intersects with our life. Regularly practiced, either alone or in a group, Bible Study helps us to understand scriptures to defend and express our faith. Consider, as I did, completing a serious study of the Bible. Bible classes for all levels of interest and ability are offered in different churches, as adult education classes, in community colleges & universities. Taking a class forced me to study, ask questions and be accountable for in-depth study; versus self study, which I would start but not complete.

Practice: BLESSING OTHERS - & giving encouragement: to think & speak well of others, to uphold them and to edify them. *Speaking positively about & appreciating others is such an easy way to build good will and leave others smiling!*

Reflection

_____

_____

_____

_____

_____

_____

C-ONNECTEDNESS – to God, to each other & to the Universe. Where do I fit in? Look around you – marvel at God's gifts to us – beginning with the miracle of ourselves and then move outward to appreciate the wonders of all of nature. Enjoy the waterfalls, rivers, mountains, prairies, hills, forests, oceans, to name just a few, and appreciate the remarkable life forms they support.

Practice: CENTERING PRAYER (CP) – an ancient *Christian method purportedly passed from Hebrew tradition in which one simply sits silently in God's presence; giving consent to love and actions within.* Some Biblical historians contend Jesus used a form of CP throughout His ministry as a means of listening to God. Centering Prayer recognizes the intrusion of thoughts – I call them 'The Committee' and gives us a way to move them to the *background, and eventually become detached from them. We sit in silence & gently release the thoughts that rise inside us to God.* It is suggested that one who has a restless and overly active mind to practice CP for 5 minutes initially and work towards a full 20 minutes sit. Simply sitting in silence & giving consent to God's presence & the actions within, is a powerful 20 minute expression of love. Daily Centering Prayer has been a life line to me & countless others, by their reports.

Divine Therapy is a fruit & benefit of continued CP & can give insights to halt self destructive behaviours. Divine therapy has been known to improve personal & professional relationships that one may have been struggling with for many years. There are many more fruits documented & explained in Fr. Thomas Keating's & others CP literature.

Practice: CONTROL OF THE TONGUE – Allow the spirit of God to partner with us to think before we speak - to change negative, hurtful words to healing, comforting words.

Practice: COMPASSION – for ourselves – for others - getting to know & caring for those that may be outsiders or disenfranchised in our community. Jesus showed care and compassion for a variety of societal outcasts and used compassion as a call to healing and restoration.

Practice: COMPOSTING – To give back to the earth God's bounty in nourishment and enrichment for the next harvest of grass, flowers and vegetables. A very satisfying way to honor our sometimes depleted earth.

Practice: COLORING AS MEDITATION – color a picture you've drawn or purchase one of the many adult coloring books available. Pick a color that represents someone or something that's on your mind and as you color, send blessings, gratitude, concerns, or wishes for recovery and happiness to the recipient of your thoughts.

Practice: CURIOSITY - maintain a childlike curiosity with self, family, community & world. Ask questions; explore new ideas, places and ways of doing things. Become slow to judge others motives or reasons for their behaviors without exploring possible causes for their way of responding. Curiosity fruits allow wisdom, knowledge, awareness and fuller appreciation of this life journey that we are taking together yet individually.

Reflection

_____

_____

_____

_____

_____

_____

**-ISCIPLINE** – to follow the path that many disciples established before us as structures to build on:

Practice: DISCERNMENT for DECISIONS; intentionally and purposefully determining what is in our best interest for healing and the courage to follow through for growth in Christ.

Practice: DREAMWORK is a process of determining what God is speaking to our heart. Practice writing down your dreams & consider consulting a Spiritual Director who can assist in interpreting the dreams. If you don't remember dreams, ask God to help remember them before falling sleep. Keep pen & paper close by bed, to write your dreams as soon as you wake.

Practice: DECLUTTER of POSSESSIONS: work to remove/clear unnecessary, unused, outgrown items for which you no longer have use. A discipline and practice that will free and prepare you for the new life God has planned for you. A wonderful way to repurpose your used items to those who have immediate use for them.

Patricia G. Johnson

Reflection

_____

**-FFORT** – needed to learn and practice Spirituality in our everyday life.

Practice: EXAMEN or Examination of Consciousness, used since ancient times (from St Ignatius of Loyola) as a means of discerning God's movement in our everyday life. The Examen involves asking each day, usually in the evening: *What has happened this day that I am most grateful for? What has happened this day that I am least satisfied with? Close with a prayer for forgiveness & grace & an resolve to correct for tomorrow.* Write your responses to determine common themes; for later reflection and possible decisions to make. There are other questions suggested to ask to determine God's movement in your life, but these two will give you a way to start using the Examen, a powerful tool for Spiritual Direction.

Reflection

_____

_____

_____

_____

_____

_____

-AITH – a belief in something not seen and yet greater than ourselves. Since we do not actually see faith, Spiritual Practices give us a tangible means to show faith and to receive faith.

Practice: FASTING – going for a period of time, usually 24 hours without solid food, drinking only water or combined with juices; a practice that helps to detox and balance the body, and mind.

Practice: FOLLOW YOUR PATH – Each of us has a path which leads to fulfillment and satisfaction in our personal and career choices. I admire those who know their path early on, yet its never too late to pivot and move to our own path. It may take a season or two of discernment to recognize the path; but it's worth the effort and possibly seeking assistance also; rather than allow disillusionment and disappointment take over our lives.

Practice: FORGIVENESS – a practice that begins healing within ourselves and strengthens our faith. When we forgive we are joining Jesus as he forgave sinners and suggested that we forgive seventy times seven. Asking Forgiveness is a powerful way of releasing negative energy and time spent in anger; often directed at ourselves and others. Simply pray,"Forgive me."

Reflection

_____

_____

_____

_____

_____

_____

**-OD,** as we know God, is at the heart of Spirituality. It has been said "God is in us and we are in God."

Practice: GRATITUDE – Thanksgiving for our lives and for all of the blessings we experience each and every day. It means giving negative attitudes a lesser role in our lives in favor of gratitude – i.e., changing our attitude to gratitude.

Practice: GRIEF – Letting go and working through the grieving process for the many losses we have experienced in our lives. Grief Groups help many to move through the phases and stages of grief with others who are sharing many of the same emotions, changes & feelings. Remember also to allow God to hold & carry you through your grief, losses & sorrow until you can stand on your own. You are not alone; the Bible tells us many times of the Great Comforter: God will never leave us nor forsake us. These reassurances are never more true & useful than in times of grief & sorrow. The grief process heals the heart & mind & changes our perspective from sadness to understanding and can lead to a gained appreciation for what we have lived through.

Reflection

_____

_____

_____

_____

_____

_____

 **-EART TALK**: Listening to what your heart yearns. What nourishes your heart, what gives you purpose and direction?

Practice: HOSPITALITY – eating, sharing food and self with others. Jesus spent many hours with his disciples and others around a table sharing prayer, food and explaining His teachings.

Practice: HAPPINESS – *The art of simply being happy & grateful for wherever we reasonably find ourselves & in whatever circumstances that are handed to us, is a personal choice, and can be learned. (Look to the history of martyrs and incarcerated innocents for examples of optimism in extreme hardships.)*

Happiness begins with an acceptance & love of ourselves & with an understanding that we have unique God-given gifts to share in all areas of our life. Developing & sharing these gifts through service can give us happiness & a deep sense of accomplishment.

Practice: HUMILITY: letting go of our desire to be known & publicly appreciated for our works. Humility means doing things for others just because it is the right thing to do, without expecting rewards or accolades. It further means letting go of pride or ownership of those qualities that can assist others.

Allow yourself to become a servant leader with a heart to match. It takes true strength & courage to reach deep & allow humility as a response to obstacles in our life. Our true self really shines through when we practice honest humility.

Reflection

_____

_____

_____

_____

_____

_____

-as the center of the universe is diminished, but not dismissed – just re-positioned.

Practice: INNER-HEALING PRAYER: working with a prayer partner who can take the healing journey with us to resolve inner wounds that keep us from fully functioning lives. Inner wounds and pain sometimes are too painful for us to face alone and yet if left alone within us will not go away and can manifest in other physical or emotional ways.

Practice: INTERCESSORY PRAYER – Praying for specific outcomes for others and ourselves. To bring specific requests related to others & ourselves is another tool to assist in turning our concerns and worries into prayer. It invites God into our care and concern for ourselves, our families, our neighbors and our entire world. No prayer is too trivial to take to God for relief.

Reflection

_____

_____

_____

_____

_____

_____

 -ESUS – the Son, the Father, and the Holy Spirit in one human form who walked among us, was unfairly judged, savagely persecuted, hung on a cross to die as a criminal and resurrected from the dead as prophesized. Jesus is epitomized and taught us through His Biblical parables on how He conducted His life. His example guides us to live in this world, not of this world. There is nothing that we will experience that Jesus has not experienced with courage & grace.

Practice: JESUS PRAYER – An anciet healing prayer used over the centuries by pilgrims, seekers, soldiers & those immersed in tedious, repetitious tasks or long treacherous journeys. The Jesus Prayer was used to get through long periods of hardships & deprivations, and is very useful today for the same reasons. Simply say or chant rhythmically, "Lord Jesus Christ, Son of God, have mercy on me a sinner". Our hardship & deprivation may include remaining clean & sober for the next minute or hour; walking a 5k; enduring a hard period of physical therapy for rehabilitation; remaining calm in the face of difficult people or circumstances; before surgery or completing a complicated project; to name a few. The Jesus Prayer has renewed my resolve many times and is the chief one I use to get me through to the other side of the situation. Try the Jesus Prayer for endurance and healing.

Practice: JOURNALING: A way of writing our thoughts, struggles, fears and feelings to God and getting feedback by reading and exploring what we have expressed before God and Jesus. No-one understands our needs and reflections quite like God, and journaling gives us a place to put emotions that may not be readily accepted by anyone else.

Reflection

_____

_____

_____

_____

_____

_____

 -NOWLEDGE – that I am loved – by God; no matter my condition and station or what I've done sustains me spiritually. Not who I am, but that I am.

Practice: KNOWLEDGE: gained by Book Study of lives of Saints and Pilgrims, both ancient and contemporary; discernment of our decisions, and attending church services. These offer a few ways to learn more to add to your spiritual knowledge base through study of God's work in others lives. They also help us to gain inspiration, by acknowledging God's love in worship and praise. Spirituality & spiritual practices will not take the place of education, knowledge, skills development or experiences, but can greatly enhance all of these qualities to help us transform to the true self we are meant to be.

Reflection

_____

_____

_____

_____

_____

_____

**-OVE:** the essential ingredient in Spirituality. The Bible teaches us because God so loved the world God gave God's only son to live among us and to teach us how to live in love. Love for God, for our self, and for others should be the cornerstone of our life. Learning to love and to be loved, is said by the ancients to be our goal and guide in life.

Practice: LECTIO DIVINA: A praying of the scriptures to learn what God is saying to us. One Benedictine method involves a four step meditation of Read, Reflect, Respond and Rest, using a portion of scripture. The Bible gives a rationale for Lectio Divina; " In the beginning was the Word & the Word was God'. There are groups available to assist with this favorite practice of mine.

Practice: LABRYINTH WALKING: an ancient way of healing, restoration & renewal that involves mindfully and deliberately walking a circular path set our so that one walks into the interior of the labyrinth, letting go of thoughts or negative emotions: spend time in the center and then walk back out, praying to take on new more positive ways for future intentions & behaviors.

One of the best known medieval labyrinths is at Chartres Cathedral, Chartres, France. Many communities and hospitals use the Chartres guide for labyrinths that are available for the patients and public to use for personal healing.

Practice: LAUGHTER: truly the best medicine to open the heart and free the mind for a brief time. Laughter releases endorphins, an essential brain hormone that gives a sense of well being and happiness. Find humor in most things daily, and you will find a different, lighter, perspective on your and others reactions, and seeming motives. Judiciously used, humor can change a most serious discussion to a manageable talk. Humor and laughter should never be at another's expense, but strive for neutral universal humor and laughter, for everyone's benefit.

Reflection

_____

_____

_____

_____

_____

_____

-EETING our personal obligations & responsibilities as a spiritual practice pays priceless dividends in the long run. This may seem simple, yet requires that we be where we say we will be, & following through with what we say we will do. To make promises and to deliver will build steps to our true self, and further build trust in us from others.

Practice: MONEY MANAGEMENT – to be debt free and living within our means is one of the most important practices we can learn. It brings powerful peace of mind to have control of our finances. There are many Biblical references to the value and joy of being faithful in small amounts, which teach us to take care of, or to be faithful, in larger amounts when it happens.

Practice: MINDFUL MEDITATION, as a way of clearing the mind temporarily of thoughts from past events & future desires while detaching from their emotional content to simply be in the present moment. This allows the mind a chance to reevaluate and make better decisions, while living in the present. To practice mindfulness is to bring self back to the present; not the past or to fantasize about the future. Simply sitting in silence for a period of 20 minutes is recommended to dismiss random thoughts as they appear, and they will appear. Learning to be mindful gives us an appreciation for the present and can save us from depression about past incidents & anxiety about the future we have no control over.

Practice: MENTORING others through the use of sharing self gained wisdom is a powerful practice. It is Biblically encouraged; beginning with Jesus to his disciples on down to present day. The building block for mentoring is that it is through the giving of self to others that we receive far more benefits than we ever give.

Practice: MIRACLE QUESTION: Ask yourself: What if I woke up tomorrow and a miracle has occurred in my life? What will have happened or changed? This simple exercise will give an indication of what we desire or wish for in our lives. Next would be to acknowledge this dream or goal and then determine: 1. Is it feasible? 2. If not feasible, why not? 3. What plans should be taken to achieve this goal? 5. What can be done today/now to start the process? This exercise can move dreams from wishful thinking to produce real changes in our lives.

Practice: MUSIC – listening to, singing, or playing an instrument brings immense personal enjoyment and takes us away from our present situation to another realm where we soar for a period of time.

Reflection

_____

_____

_____

_____

_____

_____

-**OT** an option – to ignore our spiritual needs. We ignore our spiritual needs at our own peril.

Practice: Continue to seek the best balance of Spiritual Practices for your life. It is suggested that you consider a set time each day to study & practice spiritual practices. It may involve getting up earlier each day to simply sit in silence for 20 minutes as I began doing several years ago. It is in this quiet time of the household that gives my mind the goal of calmness that lasts most of the busy day. Alternatively, you may wish to try differing times and places, just as Jesus and the disciples teach us: either indoors or outside to find your time and rhythm for spiritual refreshment. I use business travel & vacation times as opportunities to try different times & places for spiritual practices, such as Centering Prayer, pilgrimages & picking up recyclables & other trash when walking on the beach. Materials for use travel light (a phone timer, area guide & grocery bag) yet keep me mindful to respect God's space. There may be others that you try when away from home.

Practice: NON-DUAL OR NON-JUDGEMENTAL THINKING: Persons, places and things are 'not right or not wrong -they are what they are' – with no judgments attached. Judgments bring expectations, which bring perceptions of success or failure, which can bring justifications or disappointments.

Reflection

_____

_____

_____

_____

_____

_____

**-PENNESS** to change allows the flexibility for our heart and mind to get the most from our spiritual practices. We are given one chance to live this second, this minute & this day: try to make the most of this gift of life by living in gratitude.

Practice: WELCOMING PRAYER; a prayer of consent on the go – a prayer to use when we are in the middle of a stressful moment: i.e., cut off in traffic, running late, preparing for guests, talking with a difficult colleague, or unexpectedly involved in an argument with family member. It is these times that we find good reason is gone and rationalization, denial and blame take over. The welcoming prayer takes us out of the conflict and gives room for Jesus to bring reason instead of our ego; which is feeling threatened and on the verge of being emotionally out of control. We pray *"Welcome Jesus, Take away my need for security & love: Take away my need for acceptance & approval: Take away my need for control of this person or event: Take away my need to fix or change this situation."* The Welcoming Prayer allows us to begin to turn over our most basic needs and fears and allowing peace and calm to come into our bodies and minds. Courage to change comes in those moments that we let go and let God.

Reflection

_____

_____

_____

_____

_____

_____

**-RAY** always – We are guided by scripture to "continually pray"- In silence and in community.

Practice: PATIENCE – The art of calmly placing space between thoughts, feelings & actions. It includes an acceptance that we are not our thoughts that fuel feelings, that lead to actions which we do own, that may be self destructive. When we take a prayer breath to halt & understand the source of unpleasant, even dangerous thoughts, we can stop feelings of anger, revenge, jealously, rage and the concurrent actions these feelings may propel us to act out! Each day provides us with many opportunities to practice patience, through prayer breathing.

Practice: PRAYER & PRAISE– the Psalmist suggests we praise God seven times a day (Psalm 119) – Simply said, "Lord, I praise you". Practice kindness, generous spirit and thanks *for God's gifts freely given to us for others benefit. The Bible* teaches to pray always and without ceasing. We get by giving; truly priceless advice.

Practice: PILGRIMAGE – is to visit a sacred place in order to walk, pray & meditate in the footsteps & paths of earlier pilgrims & martyrs. The intent is to gain spiritual insights from the events and struggles of the sacred walk or place and to honor the lives of those remembered there. There may be shrines, monuments (natural & manmade) & relics associated with the walk that help tell the story of the original sacred happenings. The experience can be both powerful and life changing.

Many walk pilgrimages in exotic parts of the world – probably the best known is walking in Jesus' footsteps in Israel, walking and praying in all of the areas and places that Jesus walked and taught, from Nazareth to Jordan, to the Dead Sea, to the sea of Galilee and many of the villages in between. I was privileged to part of a tour of Israel called In His Footsteps, led by a Christian Palestinian who guided us to reading scriptures from the same areas that Jesus spoke them.

A visit to Vezelay, France and the Basilica honouring Mary Magdalene was also an amazing pilgrimage, that gave me a new appreciation for a lady and now restored saint who is called the 'apostles apostle'. Pilgrimages can remind us of what ordinary people have contributed greatly by extraordinary choices in their lives.

These are most powerful pilgrimages that have had a lasting impact on me and are ones I wished more could take. However, there are many sacred areas closer to home and I encourage you to explore them; from visiting beautiful churches to other sacred places related to ancient cultures and peoples. There are books and pamphlets available from your local and state communities that provide information on sacred sites to explore close to home. Pilgrimage could also be taken through readings and meditations. I encourage you to seek your own pilgrimage for spiritual growth.

Practice: PRAYER BEADS – either making or using prayer beads to remind us in a tactile way of the prayers for different days or weeks. There are prayer beads available for different religious denominations. I carry a small bracelet of prayer beads to remind me of prayer and calmness, through tumultuous times.

Practice: PRAYER TREE– An easy way to unload burdens and to raise praises for many of our blessings. I make a Prayer Tree from stripped branches, placed in a vase of your size & choice. I use a tall copper pitcher found in a flea market. Suggest attaching cut out leaves, fruit or birds with written messages of blessings, concerns or wishes for self or others. Use ornament hooks to attach the messages. Say a prayer for the tree. My Prayer Tree is strong enough to take all of my burdens and blessings. Consider taking the Prayer Tree to meditation events for others to place messages upon. A visible and powerful means to Let Go and Let God take our cares, concerns, blessings, thanksgivings and intercessory prayers.

Reflection

_____

_____

_____

_____

_____

_____

-UALITY of spirituality; in your life can be best measured by the fruits of being closer to God, by peace, joy & feelings of well being, to name a few. The many fruits of the spirit are the results of using our spiritual gifts for the building of God's Kingdom on earth.

Practice: LIVING WITH THE PRESENCE, by developing a continued openness and awareness of Christ's presence living in each of us. Remind yourself that you are living in the presence of God throughout the day; by saying "I am here" which is a reminder to move through the interruptions of the day. God is there with us and enjoys our attempting to stay connected to God, as well as assists us in many of the activities we attempt during the day. I used to hear people say they felt they had to leave God in the parking lot to keep the sacred separate from work; yet some of the most important decisions we make during the work day including customer service, presentations, negotiations, team work and persuasion for ideas should only be attempted with God' assistance. It's amazing how much more power we have when we take God into the meeting, or even into what might seem to be a friendly conversation, by simply praying just before going in. I have avoided many a minefield by praying before entering.

Reflection

_____

_____

_____

_____

_____

_____

 **-ESTING** in God's pure love – a feeling of belonging, of being home, here on earth.

Practice: RULE OF LIFE – A covenant, agreement or contract *with our Holy Spirit – an ancient monastic practice of charting our spiritual practices.* What gives you strength? What gives you joy? What motto comes to mind, when you think of life's struggles and what you may have been taught or heard words to live by? If we think about it, most of us have sayings for all aspects of managing our lives from friendships – 'to have a friend, we should be a friend' to managing our finances 'neither a borrower or lender be' to other parts of our lives. You might want to periodically reevaluate your Rules of Life and write or rewrite those that do not apply at present. It is suggested that one reevaluate and rewrite their Rules of Life on a regular basis. Rules of Life may include integrative practices that nourish our body, mind and soul that we want to elevate to our conscious level. They may include sobriety/abstinence from all mood altering substances, exercise, regular sleep patterns, recycling, staying in regular contact with friends and family, gardening, forgiveness, making amends promptly, eating less and sensibly, praying for others, regular church worship, and many more. Begin your Rule of Life with what you are doing presently to strengthen your spiritual life, and expand from there, as needed. Let your Rule of Life be personal reminders to live the life wished for yourself. Indeed the many practices in this book will apply to a Rule of Life. Your Rule of Life may be one thing listed to multiple things that will enrich your spiritual journey.

Practice: RECYCLING - Sharing your earth's bounty gifts with others. Separating items for redistribution so others might use. Providing small meals from your leftovers for single giving are small but much appreciated ways to honor out many blessings and to assist others in need.

Practice: RETREAT - *a path for reflection and renewal.* Involves getting away for a day, two days or longer or simply retreating into your own space for reflective meditations or readings. Retreats are held regularly at churches, religious centers or monasteries and the general public is invited, regardless of religious affiliations. Topics for retreats are as varied as the retreat itself from study of religious thought, people or just silence. Many are posted online for your review and information, and can be found close to where you live.

Practice: RESPECT – for self, for others, for the life and many resources God has given us. Holding all that we have and those we encounter as a sacred precious gift to cherish and carefully use with a grateful heart. Maintain a courteous response to all that happens to us, and for all who enter our daily lives.

Reflection

_____

_____

_____

_____

_____

_____

-TAYING on our spiritual course – through the good times and the rough patches; one step after the other is a noble goal to pursue.

Practices: SELF-CARE - the best way we can appreciate these bodies that are God given is to take the best care possible of ourselves. Care of our bodies involves regular checkups, exercise, dietetic concerns, spending time with friends and family and listening to our bodies and making adjustments to our schedules and requirements as needed. This is not being selfish but instead is a necessary part of taking care and honoring this precious commodity, ourselves, which we have been given by God. Self –care further involves the care of our emotional, spiritual & intellectual well being. Discernment may involve asking professionals for assistance to these important elements.

Practice: SERVICE - to practice the way of the servant leader – to be willing to serve others in ways that stretch us and to use our spiritual gifts. Ask how can I be of assistance? – and be willing to give what others ask. Plan a way to use your gifts to assist others.

Practice: SOBRIETY - practicing moderation in all parts of our life: to resolve freedom from any addiction or cravings that rule our life and which can come between us & God's love. To willingly enter a program of recovery that ensures that we live a life with our compass axis directed heavenward. Acknowledging powerlessness over an addiction is the first step in seeking help to overcome it. "God grant me the serenity to accept the things I cannot change; courage to change the things I can; and wisdom to know the difference." Reinhold Niebur.

Practice: SHADOW-WORK – getting acquainted with our Shadow, or the part of ourselves we really detest, and try to keep hidden. Shadow Work can be life changing and can reduce much of the energy of trying to keep the Shadow stuffed or repressed. To know 'who I am' includes making the sometimes uncomfortable journey to understand our conscious and unconscious motivations, defenses, and other barriers which can prevent our becoming our true self. A spiritual Director or Jungian trained counsellor can assist with this practice.

Practice: SUSPEND DISBELIEF: To avoid thinking 'you'll never be able to do that' or 'its not possible for you': to avoid critical or negative thoughts & instead visualize thoughts of positive expectations for future events to take over. To suspend disbelief allows the possibility of a different way of thinking about a situation or challenge to open for possibilities which did not seem to exist before. It may suspend fears also as faith & belief emerges to guide us to our true self. Far too often our spiritual path is blocked by fear of the unknown with possible loss of control. The Bible speaks often that "All things are possible with God". We are asked to Let Go & Let God. Letting go truly takes faith and belief in a power far greater than ourselves.

Reflection

_____

_____

_____

_____

_____

_____

-RUTHFULNESS with others means being honest about ourselves while understanding and minimizing our destructive ulterior motives and false intentions.

Practice: TRUTH-TELLING; without rationalization, exaggeration or embellishments to impress others or to make us look good. It means living with integrity and honesty in all aspects of our lives. Jesus teaches us by his life to "...let our 'yes' be 'yes' and our 'no' be 'no'; anything beyond this comes from the evil one" (Matthew 5:37).

Practice: BECOMING TRUTH AWARE when you stretch or manipulate the truth, and gratefully recognize how the Holy Spirit in your conscience calls you into check.

Practice: TAIZE – a style of singing prayer meditation that uses Bible scriptures in a repetitive singing manner, along with readings, prayers, & periods of silence. Taize is used in religious communities to collectively sing praises & gratitude or prayers of need. Taize is associated with the village Taize in Burgundy, France that started after WW II to promote healing & reconciliation throughout the world. Many churches offer Taize services as a beautiful song form of worship.

Reflection

_____

_____

_____

_____

_____

_____

-NDIVIDED ATTENTION – to our Spiritual Practices.

Practice: TO LIVE IN UNITY with our brothers and sisters from other cultures, and to reconcile other Christian denominations. When we look at others, to see God in the face of everyone. This means to refrain from saying anything divisive about other bodies of God & Christ. It also means to accept & agree on points we have in common with other religions, rather than focus on differences.

Practice: SEPARATING THE PERSON, made in God's image, from the belief that we don't/can't accept – i.e., 'I love you, yet cannot accept your actions or beliefs'.

Reflection

_____

_____

_____

_____

_____

_____

 **-IGILENCE** – Maintain awareness of our Spiritual practices as well as to our surroundings and acquaintances: to avoid toxic people and environments that do not nourish our spirit and goals, whenever possible. Relationships of any kind need not be so stressful that we dread engagement. When simply avoiding them are not an option, we have a choice to learn to make these encounters win-win for us & for them. Letting go of our egoic needs & considering others will go a long way in resolving some of the difficult & toxic relationships that we are required to maintain. Prayer for specific guidance works miracles in these situations. Consider these challenges as building blocks for character on the journey of becoming our true self.

Practice: VISIO-DIVINA – holy seeing or a way of praying with the eyes. In the church, through icons, stained glass windows, beautiful basilicas and other structures, statues, mosaics: seeing art and other items as invitations to pray and worship with the eyes. There is God's beauty in abundance throughout our world and environment that give us pause for the perfection of creation. It is all given for our appreciation and to lead us to God in gratitude. You may want to collect sacred pictures, statues and other pieces of art that invite you to pray and reflect on the beauty of God in all things.

Reflection

_____

_____

_____

_____

_____

_____

**-ORSHIP**: Paradoxically, what we consider very important and worship– may not be religious at all. Think of what motivates you, gives you inspiration to continue on and you will find what you worship; is it money, success, the ideal relationship, our children's success, the perfect vacation place, or favorite restaurant? God reveals God in worship.

Practice: WORSHIP as a way of honoring God. A necessary exercise that keeps us on our spiritual journey, and may be found only as part of our own personal spiritual journey. We are encouraged to seek and find our own worship practice, that honours God & Jesus' teachings.

Reflection

_____

_____

_____

_____

_____

_____

-**TRA** – benefits come incrementally with time and practice of Spiritual Practices. Others may notice the changes in you before you are aware of your own transformation.

Reflection

_____

_____

_____

_____

_____

_____

 **-OUR** Practices; will become your spiritual program, & your spiritual successes.

Practice: YOKE OR TEAMING - with the Holy Spirit to lighten burdens, cares and worries. Jesus invites us in Matthew 11:29-30 to yoke with him to lighten our loads. It is a beautiful image and lets us know we are not alone with our many burdens and responsibilities.

Practice: YOGA – both a meditation and a form of exercise. A way to clear our minds as we stretch our bodies. There are a variety of Yoga practices available: depending upon your level of strength and activity; from gentle Yoga to Hot Yoga. I use a Christian Gently Yoga- a form that allows time, breath and instruction for proper setups of the poses & one that uses Bible verses as motivation to hold and complete the poses.

Reflection

_____

_____

_____

_____

_____

_____

**-EN**, Simplify: Keep it manageable to Succeed and to Success!

Practice: ZENTANGLE – for all of us doodlers - a fun way to extend our doodling & prayer through a directed meditative doodling. Zentangle can be used as a way to direct prayers on anything or anyone important to us. I've known of those who use ZenTangle to interpret dreams. A talent for drawing is not required! Easy instructions for ZenTangle can be found online.

Practice: ZEST WITH INTENTION – add one practice at a time; experts say it takes 21 days to form a habit. I encourage you to try one practice for 21 days and journal your feelings and overall benefits or dislikes to determine whether to continue with the new practice. Some practices are not for everyone, but we will not know until we try if the practice benefits us or not. After all, life is a wonderful journey with many surprises along the way! I fully encourage you to begin your spiritual journey this day.

Reflection

_____

_____

_____

_____

_____

_____

Written by: Patricia G. Johnson
Began July 2017

www.ingramcontent.com/pod-product-compliance
Lightning Source LLC
Chambersburg PA
CBHW060354130626
46553CB00003B/1228